Ready, Set, GO!

Susan Canizares
Pamela Chanko

Scholastic Inc.
New York • Toronto • London • Auckland • Sydney

Acknowledgments

Literacy Specialist: Linda Cornwell

Social Studies Consultant: Barbara Schubert, Ph.D.

Design: Silver Editions

Photo Research: Silver Editions

Endnotes: Jacqueline Smith

Endnote Illustrations: Anthony Carnabucia

Photographs: Cover: Frank Pedrick/The Image Works; p. 1: Rudi von Briel/Photo Edit; pp. 2–3: Steve Powell/Tony Stone Images; p. 4: David Madison/Tony Stone Images; p. 5: Amwell/Tony Stone Images; p. 6: B. Daemmrich/The Image Works; p. 7: Frank Pedrick/The Image Works; p. 8: Jean Y. Ruszniewski/Tony Stone Images; p. 9: Joe McBride/Tony Stone Images; p. 10: Thomas Zimmerman/Tony Stone Images; p. 11: David Madison/Tony Stone Images; p. 12: Tom Raymond/Tony Stone Images.

Library of Congress Cataloging-in-Publication Data
Canizares, Susan 1960-
Ready, set, go!/Susan Canizares, Pamela Chanko.
p.cm. -- (Social studies emergent readers)
Summary: Simple text and photographs introduce different sports, including baseball, soccer, skiing, surfing, and football.
ISBN 0-439-04565-7 (pbk.: alk. paper)
1. Sports--Juvenile literature. 2. Athletics--Juvenile literature. [1. Sports.] I. Chanko, Pamela, 1968-. II. Title. III. Series.
GV704.C36 1999
796--dc21
98-53543
CIP AC

2   3   4   5   6   7   8   9   10   08   03   02   01   00   99

Ready … set …

run!

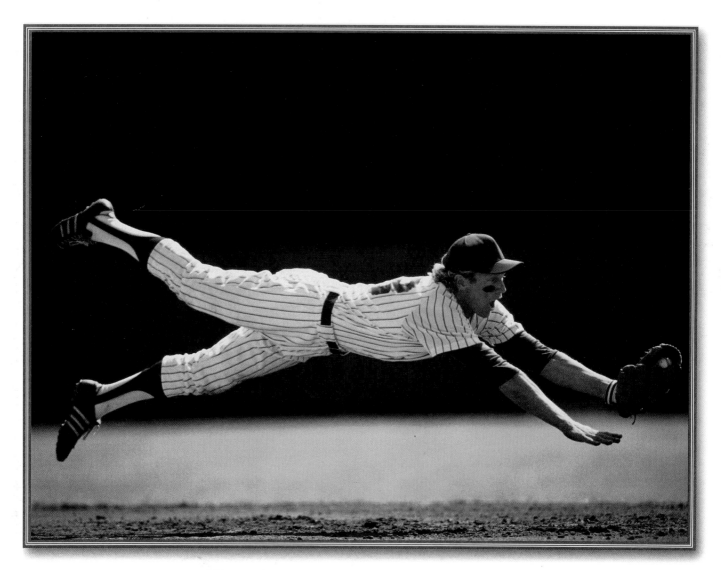

Ready, set, catch!

Ready, set, kick!

Ready, set, shoot!

Ready, set, ride!

Ready, set, ski!

Ready, set, surf!

Ready, set, row!

Ready ... set ...

go!

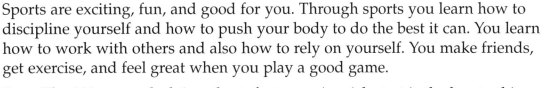

Ready, Set, Go!

Sports are exciting, fun, and good for you. Through sports you learn how to discipline yourself and how to push your body to do the best it can. You learn how to work with others and also how to rely on yourself. You make friends, get exercise, and feel great when you play a good game.

Run The 100-meter dash is a short, fast race. A quick start is the key to this race. When the starter says "On your mark," the runners crouch on all fours. At the command "Set," they lean forward with their weight on their hands. Then the pistol goes off. The runners burst forward and don't slow down until they cross the finish line! The 100-meter dash is one of a group of running, jumping, and throwing contests known as track and field sports. They are the oldest organized sports in the world.

Catch In baseball there are two teams of nine players each. The pitcher throws the ball to the batter, and the batter tries to hit it into the field with the bat. If he hits it, he runs around as many bases as he can—without letting the opposing team's players tag him "out."

Kick Soccer is the world's most popular sport. The World Cup soccer competition, which is held in a different country once every four years, is watched by more people than any other sporting event. In soccer, the 11 players of each team try to get the ball into the opposing teams' goal using their heads, feet, or body. Only the goalkeeper can use his or her hands.

Shoot Basketball is another sport that was invented in America. It was almost called boxball—a gym instructor wanted to make up a new indoor ball game and asked a janitor to hang some boxes on the wall. The janitor couldn't find boxes, nailed up two peach baskets instead, and basketball was born. In basketball two teams, of five players each, try to throw the ball into the opposing team's basket.

Ride The most famous bicycle race in the world is the Tour de France. It lasts between 25 and 30 days and goes through mountainous roads in France and neighboring countries. Over 200 cyclists attempt the 2,000-mile race every July. Only about half the people who enter finish the race.

Ski Skiers in downhill races try to go straight down the slope as fast as they can, sometimes getting up to 80 mph! That's faster than the speed limit on the highway. Downhill racing is just one kind of ski competition. Others include slalom, in which the skier must zigzag back and forth through a series of gates, and ski jumping.

Surf Hawaii is the birthplace of surfing. It is still considered one of the best spots for the sport because the waves are so tall—sometimes 30 feet high. Surfers usually stand on their surfboards and ride on breaking waves, guiding the boards with their bodies. Expert surfers can do all kinds of amazing things—even ride their surfboards standing on their heads!

Row Kayaks are narrow, usually one-person canoes that were first used by people in Arctic regions. They were originally made of animal skins over a whalebone or wooden frame. Kayaks today are made of Fiberglas or plastic. They are completely enclosed except for the snug opening through which the occupant enters and sits with legs stretched out in front. The rower uses one paddle with a double blade and dips it into the water first on side, then the other, to steer the kayak.

Go In football there are two teams of 11 players each. The object is to kick, pass, or carry the ball past the goal line and into the end zone of the other team—a touchdown! Along the way, the other teams tries to stop the player with the ball by crashing into him or jumping on top of him (called tackling). Players definitely need the protective helmets and big pads of the uniforms!